Celebrations in My World

Veterans Day

Robert Walker

Crabtree Publishing Company
www.crabtreebooks.com

Crabtree Publishing Company
www.crabtreebooks.com

Author: Robert Walker
Coordinating editor: Chester Fisher
Series and project editor: Susan LaBella
Editor: Adrianna Morganelli
Proofreader: Molly Aloian
Editorial director: Kathy Middleton
Production coordinator: Katherine Berti
Prepress technician: Katherine Berti
Project manager: Kumar Kunal (Q2AMEDIA)
Art direction: Rahul Dhiman (Q2AMEDIA)
Cover design: Sgruti Aggarwal (Q2AMEDIA)
Design: Cheena Yadav (Q2AMEDIA)
Photo research: Dimple Bhaorwal (Q2AMEDIA)

Photographs:
Alamy: Enigma: p. 30; Jeff Greenberg: p. 1
AP Photos: Rob Griffith: p. 14; Bill Haber: p. 7; Timothy F. Sosa: p. 26
BigStockPhoto: Todd Pope: p. 20
Corbis: Bettmann: p. 4, 6; James P. Blair: p. 13; Carlos Duran: p. 8; Joseph Sohm/Visions of America: p. 29
Getty Images: Darren Carroll/Sports Illustrated: p. 22; Mark Kauffman/Time & Life Pictures: p. 10; Michael Loccisano: p. 25; U.S.Coast Guard/Handout: p. 31
Istockphoto: Klaas Lingbeek-Van Kranen: p. 23
Library of Congress: p. 24
Photolibrary: Visions LLC: p. 15
Reuters: Alice Dunhill: cover; Luke MacGregor: p. 5; Ho New: p. 28; Darrin Zammit Lupi: p. 21
Rex Features: p. 9, 11, 16, 27; Stuart Clarke: p. 17; Mark Large/Associated Newspapers: p. 12
Shutterstock: folio image; Cynthia Farmer: p. 18
Other images by Digital Stock

Library and Archives Canada Cataloguing in Publication

Walker, Robert, 1980-
  Veteran's Day / Robert Walker.

MAY 2 8 2010

(Celebrations in my world)
Includes index.
ISBN 978-0-7787-4767-3 (bound).--ISBN 978-0-7787-4785-7 (pbk.)

    1. Veterans Day--Juvenile literature.
I. Title. II. Series: Celebrations in my world

D671.W34 2009   j394.264   C2009-905256-3

Library of Congress Cataloging-in-Publication Data

Walker, Robert, 1980-
  Veteran's Day / Robert Walker.
      p. cm. -- (Celebrations in my world)
  Includes index.
  ISBN 978-0-7787-4785-7 (pbk. : alk. paper) -- ISBN 978-0-7787-4767-3
(reinforced library binding : alk. paper)
  1. Veterans Day--Juvenile literature. I. Title. II. Series.

  D671.W35 2010
  394.264--dc22

                                                    2009034881

Crabtree Publishing Company
www.crabtreebooks.com   1-800-387-7650

Printed in China/122009/CT20090915

Published in Canada
Crabtree Publishing
616 Welland Ave.
St. Catharines, ON
L2M 5V6

Published in the United States
Crabtree Publishing
350 Fifth Ave.
59th floor
New York, NY 10118

Published in the United Kingdom
Crabtree Publishing
Maritime House
Basin Road North, Hove
BN41 1WR

Published in Australia
Crabtree Publishing
386 Mt. Alexander Rd.
Ascot Vale (Melbourne)
VIC 3032

Contents

What is Veterans Day? **4**

America at War **6**

Who Are Veterans? **8**

The First Veterans Day **10**

Symbols of Veterans Day **12**

Veterans Day Parades **14**

Veterans Day Services **16**

Unknown Soldiers **18**

Veterans Day and Memorial Day **20**

Special Monuments **22**

Helping Our Veterans **24**

Veterans' Organizations **26**

Veterans Day in Schools **28**

Get Involved! **30**

Glossary and Index **32**

What is Veterans Day?

Veterans Day is an annual national holiday in the United States. Veterans are people who have served in the armed forces, like the Army, Navy, Air Force, Coast Guard, and the Marines. This special day honors the men and women who have served in the American **military**. Veterans Day events are held in communities across the country.

Veterans Day is celebrated each year in the United States with parades and other **memorial** services.

● Marines carry a wounded soldier during fighting in the Vietnam War.

Many veterans will take part in Veterans Day memorial services.

Americans show their appreciation for the men and women who risk their lives in service of their country.

DID YOU KNOW?

Veterans Day is celebrated every year on the eleventh hour of November 11. This is because in 1918, World War I ended on that day.

America at War

The United States has fought in several major wars. In World War I, America fought with Britain and other countries against Germany, Austria-Hungary, and Turkey from 1914 to 1918. In World War II, America joined forces with Britain and the Soviet Union against Germany, Italy, and Japan from 1939 to 1945.

American soldiers are in the thick of battle during the Korean War.

6

Between 1950 and 1953, the United States also fought in the Korean War.

In 1964, American forces fought against North Vietnam in the Vietnam War. The United States also helped Kuwait fight Iraqi invaders in the Gulf War in 1991. Today, the United States is involved in fighting in Iraq and Afghanistan.

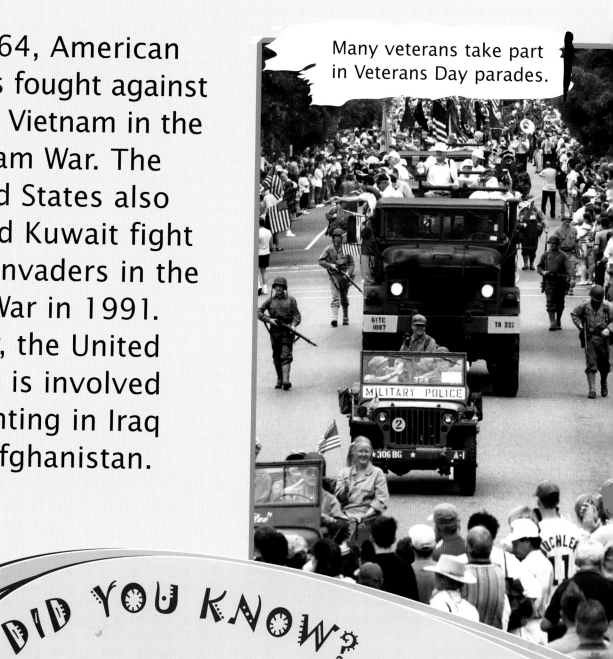

Many veterans take part in Veterans Day parades.

DID YOU KNOW?

Veterans Day is for those who have served during wars and for those who protect our country when there is peace.

7

Who Are Veterans?

A veteran is someone who has served in the United States armed forces. People in the armed forces are called service people. There are almost 25 million veterans living in America today. Veterans are men and women who have served in the military during wartime, as well as during times of peace.

The Navy is one of the branches of the United States military.

Veterans are men and women who have put themselves at risk to defend, or fight for, their country. Wars are very dangerous.

Countries use bullets, bombs, and other deadly weapons to fight one another. As a result, many veterans are injured in battle, sometimes very badly.

Former President George W. Bush, gives thanks to an American veteran.

DID YOU KNOW?

Sixteen percent of Gulf War veterans were women.

9

The First Veterans Day

The first Veterans Day was on November 11, 1918, at the end of World War I. It was called Armistice Day. Many Americans died in World War I. Armistice Day became a yearly event in the United States. After World War II, Americans wanted a day to honor all veterans, not just those from World War I.

President Dwight Eisenhower officially changed Armistice Day to Veterans Day.

In 1954, American President Dwight Eisenhower officially changed Armistice Day on November 11 to Veterans Day.

In 1968, **Congress** moved Veterans Day from November 11 to the fourth Monday in October. But many people wanted to keep the November 11 date for Veterans Day, and in 1978, it was moved back to that date.

- President Barack Obama honors the memory of America's veterans at the Bronze Soldiers Memorial.

DID YOU KNOW?

In Canada, November 11 is known as Remembrance Day.

11

Symbols of Veterans Day

Many veterans wear their military uniforms on Veterans Day.

They also wear the different **medals** they earned for serving their country. This helps people to know who veterans are at different events held on Veterans Day. It also shows how proud service people are of defending the United States.

- Parades are a special time for Americans to show their thanks to American veterans.

Homes and businesses often have American flags on display. The poppy flower is usually worn on Memorial Day, but many also wear it on Veterans Day. The poppy comes from the poem "In Flanders Fields," which tells of poppies growing among soldiers' graves during World War I.

Many children enjoy the parades during Veterans Day in the United States.

DID YOU KNOW?

Since the formation of the United States in 1776, over 48 million Americans have served in the armed forces.

Veterans Day Parades

Parades are a big part of Veterans Day. They are held in towns and cities across the country. Huge crowds of people attend, including children. There are floats, **ROTC** groups, the National Guard, bagpipes, and marching bands. Many veterans will also take part in parades.

Bagpipes are often part of Veterans Day parades.

Military vehicles like jeeps and tanks sometimes take part in Veterans Day parades. Horses are also a common sight. At some parades, military planes fly by overhead.

Soldiers are proud to march in Veterans Day parades.

DID YOU KNOW?

In the United Kingdom, people honor their veterans on the second Sunday of November, called Remembrance Sunday.

Veterans Day Services

Special services are held at military **tombs** and **monuments** on Veterans Day.

These events also attract large crowds of people who want to pay respect to service people.

- Many Veterans Day services will feature a "gun salute," where soldiers fire rifles into the air.

DID YOU KNOW?

The word "veteran" comes from the Latin "veteranus," which means 'old.'

16

There are speeches, and sometimes a "gun salute." Many veterans attend, dressed in their uniforms.

On Veterans Day, there is a moment of silence, when people pause to honor the veterans. At some Veterans Day services, the musical piece *Taps* is played on a trumpet.

Veterans Day services involve veterans from many different wars.

17

Unknown Soldiers

The Tomb of the Unknowns is a military monument or gravestone. It is dedicated to American soldiers who gave their lives in battle. These soldiers were never identified. Every year on Veterans Day, the president of the United States lays a wreath on the Tomb of the Unknowns. The Tomb of the Unknowns has been guarded all day, every day since 1937.

A wreath is laid at the Tomb of the Unknowns every Veterans Day.

A special team of soldiers take turns marching in front of the memorial, using exactly 21 steps on each trip. This stands for the 21-gun salute, which is a very special honor given by the military.

- Guards walk back and forth in front of the Tomb of the Unknowns.

DID YOU KNOW?

The soldiers who watch over the tomb are called Tomb Guards. It is one of the highest honors in the military.

Veterans Day and Memorial Day

People often confuse Veterans Day and Memorial Day. Both are national holidays dedicated to military service people. The two holidays are different, however. Memorial Day honors those who lost their lives in battle, while Veterans Day honors everyone who has served in the military.

Veterans' gravesites are often visited on Veterans Day.

Memorial Day used to be known as Decoration Day. It first began as a day to honor United States soldiers who fought in the American Civil War. For many years it was held on May 30. Memorial Day is now held every year on the last Monday of May. At 3 p.m. local time, people across the country pause for the National Moment of Remembrance.

Poppies are sold by Veterans' organizations for Memorial Day.

DID YOU KNOW?

Memorial Day was started as a way to remember the soldiers who died in the American Civil War.

21

Special Monuments

Many people visit military monuments on Veterans Day.

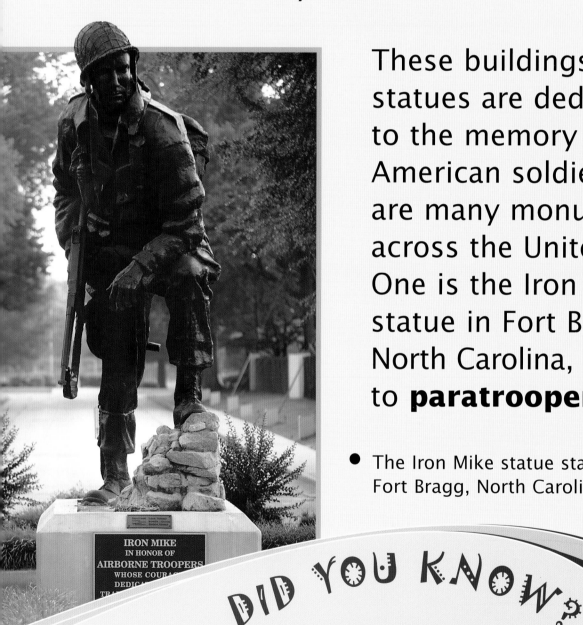

These buildings and statues are dedicated to the memory of brave American soldiers. There are many monuments across the United States. One is the Iron Mike statue in Fort Bragg, North Carolina, dedicated to **paratroopers**.

- The Iron Mike statue stands at Fort Bragg, North Carolina.

IRON MIKE
IN HONOR OF
AIRBORNE TROOPERS
WHOSE COURA
DEDICA

DID YOU KNOW?

A Korean War Veterans Memorial is in West Potomac Park, Washington, D.C.

The National World War II
Memorial is in Washington, D.C.

Some monuments, like the National World War II Memorial, in Washington, D.C., are very large and **elaborate**. The memorial has 56 pillars, two arches, a plaza, and a large fountain. The Freedom Wall, also in Washington, D.C., has over 4,000 gold stars, to honor the Americans who died in World War II. These monuments draw visitors all year long.

23

Helping Our Veterans

Near the end of the American Civil War, President Abraham Lincoln pledged to help those people injured in battle.

He gave a speech, promising "to care for him who shall have **borne** the battle and for his widow, and his orphan." Over 600,000 soldiers lost their lives in the war, and hundreds of thousands were injured.

- Abraham Lincoln worked to ensure that American veterans were appreciated and cared for.

DID YOU KNOW?

*There are almost six million veterans today with a **disability**.*

24

The Veterans Affairs Medical Center provides medical care to U.S. veterans.

Lincoln wanted to honor the huge sacrifice the soldiers made.

Lincoln's words are on plaques at the U.S. Department of Veterans Affairs in Washington, D.C. The Department of Veterans Affairs provides assistance to military veterans. It gives compensation to disabled veterans, helps with education and home loans, and provides for families of soldiers who gave their lives for their country.

Veterans' Organizations

Created in 1930, the U.S. Department of Veterans Affairs was once called the Veterans Administration. There are also many private veterans' organizations that offer support to American service people.

American veterans receive healthcare and other kinds of support.

DID YOU KNOW?

The Department of Veterans Affairs provides for the husbands, wives, and children of soldiers.

Veterans Day is a time for veterans of different wars to meet with each other.

There are many different veterans' organizations. Some are just for military who were in certain battles, or who have served in certain **branches** of the military. There are some just for members of the Air Force and some only for marines. Many of these organizations work to improve the support veterans receive from the government.

Veterans Day in Schools

Many schools have special activities on Veterans Day. Some have Veterans Day assemblies, with speeches and other performances in honor of American veterans. At many schools, students say the Pledge of Allegiance, play patriotic music, and observe a moment of silence.

Speaking with veterans helps students appreciate the **sacrifices** they have made.

Many veterans are willing to come into classrooms and to speak to students. This is a wonderful way for students to learn firsthand about veterans and the amazing sacrifices they make in service of their country.

A Boy Scout troop honors veterans' graves at Arlington National Cemetery.

DID YOU KNOW?

In 2001, November 11-17 was designated as National Veterans Awareness Week. It encourages learning about veterans in schools.

Get Involved!

There are many ways for you to honor American veterans. You could volunteer at a Veterans Affairs hospital, help out with veterans' fundraisers, or write a "thank you" letter to someone in the military.

A veteran reads a handmade card.

DID YOU KNOW?

In 1862, President Lincoln approved the Medal of Honor to be given to soldiers who showed special bravery in battle.

Many classes make "thank you" cards and posters for soldiers on Veterans Day.

There are also plenty of fun Veterans Day games and activities you and your friends can do. Better yet, you could go to your local library and read about veterans in one of the hundreds of books on the subject. We should all take part in this very important national holiday.

Glossary

borne To have carried out their duty

branches The different parts

Congress The law making part of the American government

disability An injury or handicap

elaborate Many parts

medal An award

memorial A ceremony or building that reminds people of something

military The armed forces

monument A statue or building

paratrooper A solider who uses a parachute to drop into battle

ROTC Reserve Officers' Training Corps

sacrifice Giving up something to help

tomb A place to bury the dead

Index

Afghanistan 7

armed forces 4, 8, 13

Armistice 10, 11

Civil War 21, 24

families 25

flags 13

holidays 4, 20, 31

Iraq 7

Lincoln, Abraham 24, 25, 30

medals 12, 30

memorial 4, 5, 11, 13, 19, 20, 21, 22, 23

military 4, 8, 12, 15, 16, 18, 19, 20, 22, 25, 27, 30

monuments 16, 18, 22, 23

parades 4, 12, 13, 14, 15

poppies 13, 21

uniforms 12, 17

Vietnam 4, 7

war 4, 6, 7, 9, 10, 13, 21, 23, 24

wreath 18